DEAR GOD

DEAR GOD

Children's Letters to God

DAVID HELLER

Illustrated by John Alcorn

ANGUS
& ROBERTSON
PUBLISHERS

ANGUS & ROBERTSON PUBLISHERS

16 Golden Square, London W1R 4BN,
United Kingdom, and Unit 4, Eden Park,
31 Waterloo Road, North Ryde, NSW, Australia 2113

First published in the United Kingdom
by Angus & Robertson (UK) in 1988

Copyright © David Heller 1987

Typeset by New Faces, Bedford
Printed by Hazell Watson & Viney, Aylesbury

British Library Cataloguing in Publication Data
Dear God.
    1. Christian doctrine. God – Children's
    viewpoints – Collections
    I. Heller, David
    231

ISBN 0 207 15924 6

Dedicated to a God of
Mirth & Kindness:
I Have Faith That YOU
Know How To Take A Joke

Contents

Introduction

When I was five years old or so, there was an afternoon television show called 'House Party,' which sometimes featured children talking about almost anything under the sun. The popular theme of the show was: 'Kids say the darnedest things!' I remember watching the program faithfully. I really liked watching other children on TV, but for all my half decade of life experience I could not figure out what was so funny about them. Now, some twenty-three years later, I believe I understand. Children really tell the truth about life and they do it in a lovable and endearing way. As I have been exploring children's ideas about God and about the world, I have come to realize that kids not only say the 'darnedest' things, they say the wisest things as well.

At the same time that I was intrigued with children on television, I was also beginning to learn about religion and my heritage. Growing up in a Jewish family, I was a child surrounded by ritual and history at an early age. Candle lighting was as familiar to me as catching a baseball; prayer was as much a part of my routine as riding a bicycle. But I was also the child of a Holocaust survivor, and this legacy created a special and sometimes formidable challenge for me.

As a child I thought as a child, but I was drawn to the global concerns of adults. I wanted to make sense of how people acted, and I was especially curious about belief and doubt in a God. I asked many questions of nearby grown-ups, local clergy, and teachers as well as my parents. 'Why is the world the way it is?' I asked with tireless persistence. I received many different answers, as most children do, and I kept searching. A few years later, I became one of the first Jews in a private, Jesuit Catholic high school. This experience, particularly the close relationships I developed with faculty and friends, continued my fascination with the religions of the world. By 1984, after studying psychology and religion at Harvard and Michigan, respectively, the topic of children's God images formally became a part of my life. It was then that I began writing *The Children's God*, a book published in 1986 by the University of Chicago Press.

Writing this book helped me to understand other people's religious views as well as my own. Through my research for the book, I found that children share many ideas about God despite their differences in religion, age, and gender. Most children are concerned with how powerful God is and whether God will be a significant force in their lives. They believe that God is all around, in the sky, in flowers, and in people too. They talk a great deal about 'the God in people'. These small theologians express clear interest in their spiritual relationship to their neighbors. They seem to conclude that God created the human race with a purpose in mind, and that we are all connected to that purpose and to each other. As twelve-year-old Tamara described, 'It's all woven together ... All of our lives ... And God is at the center of our world, guiding our destiny.'

This book also compelled me to consider more closely my own personality and childhood, as each of my child interviewees opened up to me. I was consistently amazed at how the children's unique personalities influenced their images of God. There are those children who imagine a benign, helping figure – youngsters who picture a 'Dr God, the Therapist.' Eight-year-old Mike writes in his letter:

> Dear God,
>   I fell off my bike last week. My leg still hurts a lot. Could you speed up the get well work?
> > Thanks,
> > Mike

There are other children who envisage God as a congenial playmate – boys and girls who depict 'God, the Friendly Ghost'. Seven-year-old Mary provides an illustration:

> Dear God,
>   Thank you for the doll house last Christmas. I wonder if you could stop by to play with me? We could play Family, or School or maybe Bible Stories. Whatever you like.
> > Love,
> > Mary

I find myself learning something new from each of these children, because each of their God images reveals some special quality or outlook. They take me back to a simpler time, yet their interpretations cause me to think a little deeper. Their images remind me that religious belief is indeed a very personal thing and that greater acceptance of religious differences must be a continual pursuit.

While children's ideas about God should be seriously considered, they can also be lightheartedly enjoyed. While I was completing *The Children's God*, I collected a great variety of original drawings, stories, conversations and letters. I was particularly moved by the children's letters. I also received mail from parents of a variety of religious backgrounds, including devout churchgoers and atheistic parents. They were simply responding to my work with children and wanted to offer a letter or an anecdote. The humor and vitality that leaped forth from so many of their children's original and spontaneous ideas was undeniable. I found myself collecting more letters from other children and sharing the letters with friends and relatives, including my thirteen-year-old and ten-year-old cousins. Adults and children alike seemed to lose themselves in what can only be described as 'a childlike sense of wonder and laughter'. I knew I must share this colorful parade of letters with a larger audience. One by one, the children's letters provide inspiration for all of us.

Children write to God about all different kinds of things. Full of curiosities, dreams, and stories to tell, children have a wonderful knack for sharing their innermost thoughts in their letters. Some children write at length about everyday concerns – about mom and dad, brothers and sisters, school activities and challenges, and the ups and downs of friendship and play. Family themes are especially vivid since parents play the primary role in helping to develop a child's God image. Some youngsters write to God about the world at large – about international troubles and national leadership, the way men and women act with each other, and those sometimes fuzzy ideas we get from television and movies. Even more than when I was a child in the 1960s, the media seems to have a profound influence on children's notions of good forces and bad forces, heroes and supernatural characters. But some children are even more reflective. They're sincerely curious about really 'hard-to-explain' things – like science, nature and religious belief and doubt. The teachings of the Bible and established religions are frequently apparent in the letters, though these formal influences tend to emerge in humorous and even exaggerated ways. Whatever an individual child's interests, we can be certain that he or she will be quite outspoken and animated – for that is what childhood is all about.

For me, personally, there have been quite a few stops on the journey from curious child to curious interviewer of children. Yet some things have remained the same: religion conveys for me a great joy and lightness of spirit and children are the ideal messengers of that spirit. They create a house party whenever they speak or write. Their special guests, those characters and images which capture their interest, are limited only by the outer reaches of a child's imagination. As you read on, you will meet some familiar and modern guests like Superman, Mr T and Ronald Reagan. But you'll also be greeted by some age-old figures like Santa Claus, Moses and those distant relatives of us all, Adam and Eve. So please join me in enjoying the timeless spirit of children. It is my considerable pleasure to pass along their letters to God and share with you their sweetness.

David Heller
Boston, Massachusetts

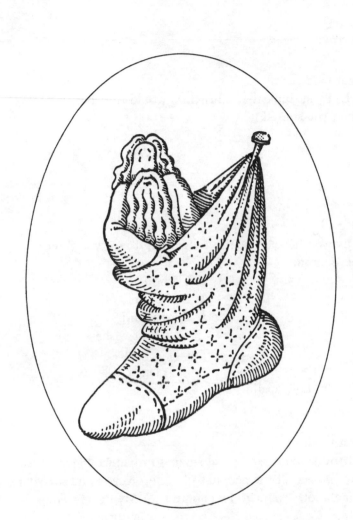

'Did You Think That
Christmas Would Turn Out
like This When You Started It?'

Dear God,
  Did you think that Christmas would turn out like this when you started it?

                              Love,
                              Wendy
                              [aged 7]

Dear God,
  Do you have a favorite religion? I'll give you three to choose from –
                    1. Catholic
                    2. Lutheran
                    3. Episcapalin
                              Best wishes,
                              Charles
                              [aged 10]
P.S. I'm Episcapalin

Dear God,
  I think you must be real smart to invent religion. That way you get all the people to look up to you and say your name a lot. I want to be famous too. My name's Frank.
                              Yours truly,
                              Frank ✿ ✿ ✿
                              [aged 11]

God,
What's the story? Why did you make the Jews stay in the desert for 40 years?
>
> Keith
> [aged 7]

Dear God,
In school, I drew a picture of Jesus and the 12 disciplens. If you want to see my drawing, stop by my house at 7 tonight.
>
> Love,
> Jennifer
> [aged 9]

Dear God,
You're my favorite God. I don't have anybody before you. I praise you a lot. I hope you will write me back and think of me always. Call me if you want.
>
> Love,
> Jerry
> [aged 9]

Dear God,
How old are you? If that Noah story is right, you must be older than my neighbor, Mr Grubb – and he's really old.
>
> Tammy
> [aged 8]

Dear God,

Can't you make church more fun? What about having a few videos?

Just trying to help,
Celia
[aged 10]

Dear God,

Why did you give Jesus such a hard time? My dad is rough on me too. So I know what it's like. Maybe you both could ease up?

Mark
[aged 11]

Dear Mr God,

Do you have a few minutes? I have a few things to say. First, thank you for the bike for Christmas. Second, thanks for the snow. Third, how about more holidays?

Sincerely,
Angela
[aged 9]

Dear God,

Who do *you* pray to? If you don't say prayers, do you think you can let me off the hook?

Jim
[aged 9]

Dear God,
   I love you. I just want to let you know ahead of time that I'd like to be there with you in heaven.
                                        Love always,
                                        Sarah
                                        [aged 8]

Dear God,
   Why is the cross **✝** the thing you chose for religion?
   We (my friend Jody and me) think you should have tried something different.
   How about something like this? ⊗⊗
                                        Pearl
                                        [aged 11]
We hope no one has used this before.

Dear God,
   What religion are the people in London.
   Have they got Christianity yet?
                                        Anna
                                        [aged 8]

Dear God,
   I just learned how to spell R E L I G I O N .
   I feel good. Now I am learning something else that we are. It is called P R E S S B U T A R R I U N .
                                        Emily
                                        [aged 6]

Dear God,

What do you *really* think about atheists? I think that you must feel like I feel about the Yankees – I hate them.

Tom

[aged 9]

Dear God,

I'd like to make a suggestion, if that's okay. Why don't you have fewer religions so people would get along better? We just read about the Crusades a long time ago.

Janet

[aged 11]

Dear God,

What do you think about people who convert? My mum says they're stupid. But the way, I like being Jewish.

Love,

Amy

[aged 10]

Dear God,

How did you get to know Mary?

Andy

[aged 6]

'Is Jesus Your Oldest Kid?'

Dear God,

My dad got laid off last week at work. Please help him find work quick.

He bugs us a lot when he is home.

Thank you,
Martin
[aged 8]

Dear nice god,

I feel close to you. Like you and I are part of the same family.

Maybe we could get married and make it easier.

Your lover,
Tina
[aged 7]

Dear God,

My grandma died a year ago. My mom says she is with you. Could you give her this letter?

Here is the letter:

Grandma, I'm doing good in school and I met a boy I'm going to marry.

All my love,
Cindy
[aged 8]

Dear God,

Thank you for my parents, my sister Anita, and for my grandma and grandpa. They are all real warm and special. I forgive you for my brother Phil.

I guess you didn't finish working on him.

Sean
[aged 12]

God,

My father reads to me from your book all the time. I like times when he does.

The Joseph character is interesting.

Love,
Joe
[aged 10]

Dear God,

Do you have an extra plague for my sister. Like you did to the Egyptians.

She's really stupid.

Stanley
[aged 8]

Dear God,

My mom is Jewish and my dad is Catholic. My mom says this makes us even more special. Two is better than one.

Do you like to mix things up like this?

See you on all the holidays.

Love you,
Beth
[aged 9]

Dear God,
   My dad thinks he is you. Please straighten him out.
                              Wayne
                              [aged 11]

Dear God,
   My mom is acting weird because she is getting old. Can
you take back a few gray hairs? That would help bring the
house back to normal.
   Thanks for what you can do.
                              Mike
                              [aged 9]

Dear Mr and Mrs God,
   What's your family like? Is Jesus the oldest?
                              Karen
                              [aged 7]

Dear God, Esq.
   My family, the Sandersons, is pleased to invite your
family, the Gods, over for bread and wine (I figured you
might like this).
   You are hereby invited on November the 3, at 7 pm.
   Please respond in writing or on a tablet by this date.
                              Very truly yours,
                              Sheila Sanderson
                              Host
                              [aged 11]

Dear God,
   Are you in charge of babies?
   I have three sisters, which is good. But I would like to put in an order for a brother.
   I hope this special order won't upset you.
                                              Love,
                                              Stuart
                                              [aged 9]

Dear God,
   Was there anything special about Bethlehem, or did you just figure that was as good a place as any to start a franchise?
                                              Your friend,
                                              Jim
                                              [aged 12]

Dear God,
   Was there really a Garden of Eden?
   My family has a garden too. But it is small and crummy. It just has a few rotten vegetables.
   Don't tell my mother I said this please.
                                              Larry
                                              [aged 10]

Dear Father of the universe,
   Since the whole galaxy is yours you must have a great family barbecue!
                                              Invite me.
                                              Chip
                                              [aged 11]

Dear God,

Thank you for giving me to a loving and caring family. That was a choice that was a good one.

By the way as long as I'm writing to you. Was there other families that you tried out first?

Tito
[aged 10]

To God,

If everybody in the whole world is related to everybody else, then how can people get married?

Let's see if you answer that one.

Pia
[aged 8]

Dear God,

My mom and my father are divorced. For 3 years.

Nobody's perfect. But why did you pick us? I wish we were all with each other.

Maybe you could have them get along on weekends.

Please,
Stephen
[aged 11]

Dear God,

I learned in school that you can make butterflies out of caterpillars. I think that's cool. What can you do for my sister? She's ugly.

Please don't tell my parents I wrote you.

Greg
[aged 11]

'Do You Spend Your Spear Time
with the Israelites, God?'

Dear God,

Be my friend? It won't cost you nothing and you don't even have to perform too many miracles.

William
[aged 8]

Dear God,

I think that you are swell. My priest said that we are wrong if we think that you are only in the clouds. He says you are here on earth too.

If it is okay with my mother, would you like to come over to dinner on Tuesday night?

We are having lasagne!

Hope you can make it,
Madelyn
[aged 9]

Dear God,

I feel that Jesus is a friend of mind. Since he's your friend too, that makes us friends. Right or not? Let's get together to play sometime. You can bring all the toys you have and I'll bring mine. We'll see who has more.

Love,
Lori
[aged 7]

Dear God,

On earth as it is in heaven. You and my friend Cindy are the best.

Love,
Carol
[aged 10]

Dear God,

My girlfriends and I started the God Fan Club. Would you like to buy a button? We're going to make them ourselves.

Just so you know, here are the members so far.

Tracy, Mary, Me, Lynn, Paula, and You

Love, Sue
[aged 8]

Long Distance to GOD:

I hope that you are well . . .

And taking care of the world. Please make us friendly with all the Arabs, with the eastern peoples and with the Africaners.

And please, this is important. Make me friends with Johnny Martins. We do not get along.

Alphonse
[aged 10]

Dear God,

O hello God. I love music and so do my friends. We sing in the church choir together. Please make sure we always stay friends. Help us to sing better.

Judith
[aged 11]

Dear God,

Why couldn't anyone in Israel get along in the Bible? There was always stone throwing and fighting. Jake, Joseph, Abe, Moses – you name them. No person was the friend of another. That's no good.

Roy
[aged 10]

Dear God,

Who was Mohammed? Was he a friend of yours like Jesus?

Also, were Moses and Joshua friends or just business partners?

I'm taking a class on religions,
Fanny
[aged 12]

Dear God,

I am having fun and making friends. Dave is talking to me about things you do and say. But I told him. How should

I know? Ask my friend George. He gets A's in school and I get C's!

> Sorry,
> Joe
> [aged 9]

Dear God,
    You are a good friend to me when I am in need.
    Like maybe now. I am broke.

> Howard
> [aged 12]

Dear God,
    Best regards. I am going to go play with my girlfriends after this. I am going to tell them about the stuff I just talked about and about the banner and pencils that the man gave me.
    If you told him what to buy for the kids, thank you. You have good taste.

> Heather
> [aged 9]

Dear God,
    I found out that I have to get glasses. I am worried about what my friends will say. They may tease me and say 4 eyes. Please make sure they do not.
    I am not vain or anything.

> Carmen
> [aged 9]

Dear friendly God,
    I think you are like a regular person.
    I do not believe those people who say you are dead or far away.
    You probably live on the next street.

                                    Marcy,
                                    [aged 8]

Dear God,
    I just made a new friend today.
    His name is Dave Heller. He is white and I am black but that is fine.
    We both love basketball.

                                    Love,
                                    Bill
                                    [aged 9]

Jesus,
    You and me is tight.

                                    I luv you,
                                    Richard
                                    [aged 6]

To God,
    Who do you spend your spear time with?
    The Israelites?

                                    Ken
                                    [aged 12]

*'Do You Watch All of Us People
on a Big TV Screen?'*

Dear GOD,
I think there is much too many things about money these days. Especially on television.
You should take some money away from people so it would not be such a big deal.

> Don't tell them
> who gave you the idea,
> Susie
> [aged 7]

Dear God,
I see President Reagan on TV all the time. He is always waving and smiling.
You should get your own station too. That way every person will know who you are and what you look like. Just like President Reagan.

> I say good prayers.
> Marianne
> [aged 9]

Dear God,
You must be very big. Like William the Refrigerator Perry.

> Love,
> Mary
> [aged 9]

Dear God,

Do your kids watch cartoons on Saturdays? Or are they helping you get ready for church on Sunday?

Your friend,
Ted
[aged 7]

Hey, God,

Do you know how in commercials they say they are going to take a break to bring us a word from the sponsor?

Well you should do that with people in their homes because you are everybody's sponsor. That would be neat. That way you could comunicate with the people.

Riley
[aged 12]

Dear God,

Is Krypton a real place?
Maybe it is just a place in Hollywood.

Frank
[aged 9]

Dear God,

What do you think about all those movies about you around Easter time? I think they're kind of corny, myself.

Your buddy,
Charles
[aged 9]

Dear God,
   Is Mr T on your side or the other side?
                                Love,
                                Hank
                                [aged 10]

Dear God,
   Can't you do something about all the bad news on TV? I
always change the chanell.
                                Cindy
                                [aged 7]

Dear God,
   I wonder if you could help me out. My mom and dad said
I can't watch TV for a week. So I guess I'm going to miss all
those religious shows, unless you do something. How about
putting in a good word for me?
                                Love,
                                Matt
                                [aged 7]

Dear God,
   They could have more bible stories on TV. I recommend
the King Solomon story, Moses, Jesus, and the lady who
turned into salt.

The Flood might make it difficult. It would be hard to show and the kids might not watch. Plus there would not be enough parts for people. Just animals.

With love,
Roberto
[aged 9]

Dear God,
What do you think about the Olympics? Don't you think all the countries should go? When they are on TV I watch all of them. Even the dancing and the speeches.

Try to watch the next one. You might like it. It will be in a place called Soul in 1988.

Love,
Jack
[aged 12]

Dear God,
A lot of folks say there is too much rough stuff on TV and too much killing too.

I say there is too much rough and tough stuff and killing in the Bible.

Derek
[aged 11]

Dear God,

I was watching TV when the Challenger shuttle exploded. That was a sad thing.

Was there anything that you could have done? Were you mad because they came too close to your territory?

We're sorry,
Jose
[aged 11]

'There Isn't Any School
in Heaven, Is There?'

Dear Jesus,

How did you learn all that stuff in the Book by Luke without going to school much?

Sharon
[aged 7]

Dear God,

I read about Abraham in school. Why did you give him such a hard time before you let him become a teacher?

The teachers here got it easy.

Barry
[aged 9]

Dear God,

You don't have to spell real good to get into heaven, do you?

My teacher told us that when we meet St Peter we have to spell a word like exagarate. If you get it right, you go to heaven. If you're wrong, you do down stairs.

I don't mean the principils office.

Sincerely,
Dom
[aged 10]

Dear New Testament God,

Since you like to write so much, maybe you could write

my current events term paper for me. It could be about anything – even you!

I am desparate,
Raymond
[aged 12]

Dear God,
The World Series starts on Tuesday. School is in the way. One of them has to go.

I vote school. Can you make it snow even if it is the start of October?

Pete
[aged 10]

Dear God,
Did you invent maths to count the animals on Noah's ark? Do we still need it?

Jeanne
[aged 11]

Dear God,
Help. I have a favor to ask you. Mr Arene teaches us. He is pretty strictly mean. I think he does not go to church either.

I wonder if you could send Jesus or an angel down to talk with him. Maybe I could invite Jesus in for my history project. That way Mr Arene won't expect anything.

End of letter,
Orson
[aged 12]

Dear God,
   Hi from School. No message.

                         Love,
                         Carla
                         [aged 6]

Dear God,
   My mom says that I can only stay out after school till it gets dark.
   My question is: Can you make the sun stand still?
   I figured if you did it once you could probably do it again.
                         Freddie
                         [aged 11]

Dear God,
   Did Matthew and John have to go to college?
                         Art
                         [aged 10]

Dear God,
   I love school and I try my best all the time. I also say my prayers every night.
   I hope this counts when it's my turn to be judged.
                         A good Christian,
                         Gloria
                         [aged 11]

God and who all is listening,
 MAKE SCHOOL ONLY AN HOUR A DAY!
                                    A good student
                                    [aged 7]

Dear God,
 Did you make pencils and pens just like you made men
and girls.
 I think pencils and pens go together better.
                                    Charles
                                    [aged 12]

Dear heavenly father (God),
 I pray to you each and every night. Sometimes I pray to
you during Science – this is not good for my grades.
                                    Davida
                                    [aged 11]

Dear God,
 I hate gym. I bet Sarah and Rachel and Becky did not
have to do gym stuff in the Bible.
 Boy those were the days.
                                    Love and prayers,
                                    Noami
                                    [aged 10]

Dear God,

When you threw Adam and Eve and all the others out of the garden, that must be when you started to have schools. You must have been plenty mad.

Hope this gives you a
laugh,
David
[aged 9]

Dear sweet and friend God,

I am being very good. I am good to my mom, my dad, my brother Bill, and my sister Elizabeth. I am nice to my friends like you. I am nice to my grandma and grandpa too.

I am *even* nice to my teachers. I try to forgiving them for being so boring.

Love,
Kristen
[aged 8]

Dear God,

I am going to begin junior high next year. You helped me make it so far. Do not leave me now!

Please,
Les
[aged 12]

Dear God,

I would like to know if you are like the principal of a school and all the presidents and kings are like teachers.

Andrea
[aged 7]

Dear God,

I am doing police for you.
My english teacher, Mrs Clayburn, has pointed ears.
I think she is Satin.

George
[aged 8]

Dear God,

We read that you made a bush burn to the ground and you did not use matches. Wow. I would like to see this done to my school.

Timmy
[aged 10]

GOD
1 NORTH POLE
EARTH 7777

How is it up there where you are?
I learned about you in geography. Say hi to Santa Claus.

Bea
[aged 9]

Dear God,

We learn about you a lot in Sunday school. We heard that you don't like temples with money in it and that you don't like Romans much either.

Who do you like?

Signed Bill,
[aged 10]

Dear God,

How far did you get in school?

I stayed back last year and I am worried.

Tyler
[aged 10]

Dear God,

Thank you for helping the poor people all around the world and for helping to educate them too.

That must be hard work. Do your kids help or are they too busy doing their homework?

Love,
Cherie
[aged 10]

Dear God,

Do you have schools in heaven or are the angels and servants born smart?

Doris
[aged 11]

'Is There a Special Place in
Heaven for Cabbage Patch Kids?'

Dear God,

Hockey is pretty tough but I love it.

I always say a prayer for all the players' injuries after the games.

Kevin
[aged 12]

Jesus,

I feel very near to you.

I feel like you are beside me all the time.

Please be with me on Thursday. I am running in a 3 mile race then. I will need all the speed in the world.

If you are not busy with other things, maybe you could be at the starting line, the finish line, and everywhere in between.

Frankie
[aged 11]

Dear God,

Were you a BOY Scout? I am.

Did you ever camp out in the desert and play jokes on people in the Bible. I bet you did.

We do all the time and have a blast.

Nat the rat
[aged 10]

Dear God,

I am fond of you. No question about it.

I love to cook. Today, I would like to make something for You. How about an omelette with bread and butter. I'll put lots of cheese in it.

Do you eat bacon? I don't know since I am a Christian. You might be kosher or something.

Love,
Melissa Sue
[aged 11]

Dear Dear Dear God,

I see you in my dreams all the time.

I know it is you because you have a crown on and you are always fishing.

Say hello next time.

Love,
Craig
[aged 9]

Dear God,

If you think it was cool the way Jesus walked on the water, you should watch me water ski!

Steve
[aged 12]

Dear Jesus,

Since you retired two thousand years ago what kinds of things do you do?

Maybe you should try bowling or you could sing in a church group like my grandmother does.

Pam
[aged 9]

Dear God,

My mom tells me a story about you every night. Last night she told me about how you always remember your mother on her birthday. And you give her divine gifts.

I think she was kidding me and herself.

Love,
Holden
[aged 7]

Dear God,

Do you have toy spaceships and things like that? That must be fun, but hard to keep track of.

You should always put your toys away when you are done.

Randy
[aged 8]

Dear God,

Was building car models big when you were a kid? Or whatever they called you.

Warren
[aged 7]

Dear God,

Do you have a special place for Cabbage Patch kids in heaven? Are they closer to you because they come from nature?

Angela
[aged 8]

Dear God,

I like to read a lot. We read *The Great Gatsby* in school. Do you have time to read? I bet you like religious books and biographies.

Please write back,
Terry
[aged 12]

Dear God,

I have a big collection of dolls. Sometimes I play Bible with them. I have them act your stories. Once I had them do the ten plagues. Then I had them go in the desert. I was not too rough on them.

Charlotte
[aged 9]

Dear God,

Do you ever get bored? I do. Do you get into trouble then? Is that why you started thunder and rain?

Let me know,
Paula
[aged 11]

Dear God,

Want to hear a joke? What is red, very long, and you hear it right before you go to sleep? Give up? Answer is a *sermon*.

Your friend,
Frank
[aged 11]

Dear God,

I just learned how to play chess. Does the earth look like a chessboard to you?

Libby
[aged 11]

God,

I need to confess. I am sorry but I looked at my older brother Eddie's *Playboy* magazine. I didn't really like it though.

Sorry,
George
[aged 10]

Dear God,

I just want to say hi! And thanks for all the people you are helping who are starving.

I'm okay here. But there is one thing. I love tennis very much and it is hard to get a court around here. Can you build some more in my neighborhood?

Thank you,
Erica
[aged 8]

Dear God,

Art is my favorite subject. I want to draw you a picture of you. Here goes.

I need to work on details. It would help if you could come down so that I could get a look at you.

Michael
[aged 7]

Dear God,

I love to eat. Thanks for all the food. Pizza was the best idea you had.

Ralph
[aged 7]

'What Did Adam and Eve
Do for Fun?'

Dear God,

What is the rest of the story about when you made boys and girls? There must be a reason why you made two different brands of people.

Hank
[aged 6]

Dear God,

My daddy says you must have a good sense of humor. That's why you created Joan Rivers and Boy George.

Love,
Ellen
[aged 9]

Dear God,

When do you think it's okay to start dating? How old were you when you went out with Mrs God? Did you kiss her on the first date?

Cheryl
[aged 10]

Dear God,

Do you think there's enough love these days? I feel there's a shortage.

Love,
Ken
[aged 9]

Dear God,

I go to a Catholic school. The priests there are very nice. But did you ever think of giving these men different clothes. I think the nuns can stay the same.

Curious,
Mary Jo
[aged 10]

Dear God,

How involved do you get in marriages? Do you give the couples any time alone?

Just asking,
Wayne
[aged 12]

Dear God,

I went to my cousin's wedding last week. I heard that you were there. I must have missed you. Do you get to all the weddings or do you just pick some? You must eat a lot of cake.

Love,
Alexandria
[aged 10]

God,

I am a nice girl. I am glad I am not a boy. They are ugly.
Only Jesus was nice.

Love,
Andrea
[aged 6]

Dear God,

What do you think of people who act sexy? I think they
are kidding themselves. It is better to act like you really are.

I try to act religious. I do my best.

Brandon
[aged 9]

Dear God,

When you made love was it hard to plan?

Is that why girls and guys act so goofy when they go out?

With many times love,
Brett
[aged 9]

Dear God,

I read about Miriam and Moses. Boy she was a good sister
to him.

I hope that he appreciated her. Some men don't.

Amy
[aged 10]

Dear God,

I'm writing to complain about how men get the biggest say in everything. I want this to stop. Now.

I want to be President some day and things are going to change. We're going to need a tornado or hurricane or something.

> I will let you know,
> Linda
> [aged 11]

Dear God,

Why do boys like dirt so much? I think it might have been better if you got the people out of the desert sooner.

> Candy
> [aged 8]

Dear God,

Do women in heaven dress up and wear makeup or are they just down to earth people?

> Wendy
> [aged 10]

Dear God,

Why do men and girls always fight? Did you believe that the earth would be more interesting that way?

> John
> [aged 8]

Dear God,

When Jonah was in the whale was it a he whale or a she whale? I think girls are probably fatter.

Mike
[aged 7]

Dear God,

I'm glad that you are a man. If you were not, you might not have made boys.

I am a boy,
Darren
[aged 10]

Dear God,

I think if you were a woman you would be more involved with domestic things like cooking and cleaning. And sewing.

Karen Ann
[aged 9]

Dear God,

I read about how Delilah cut Samson's hair. Is that why there are so many female hairdressers?

Warren
[aged 10]

God,
What did Adam and Eve do for fun? My mom said they played with toys and ate but I know better.

> Chris
> [aged 9]

Dear God,
Girls are weird. Except for my mom.

> Timmy
> [aged 7]

Dear God,
Why do we always have to let the girls go first? I bet they did not want to go first when the Christians were killed in the stadiums.

> Carl
> [aged 10]

Dear God,
When you were small, did you always listen to your mom? Women think they know everything but they do not.

I bet if you listened you would not be so big and powerful today. That is a fact.

> Bryn
> [aged 9]

Dear Ms God:

I believe that you are a woman. In fact I am sure for sure. I think that is why the rivers and sky and birds are so beautiful.

If by some fluke you are a boy please do not take it out on me. Boys should not hit girls.

Trisha
[aged 11]

'Volcanos Are Cool, But You Should Watch Your Temper, God!'

Dear God,

Do angels do carpentry and plumbing in the sky? If you don't have to be too handy, I would like to apply.

Yours,
Carmen
[aged 8]

Dear God,

I used to want to be astronaut. But I'm not sure it's safe anymore. What's the weather report?

Kevin
[aged 12]

Dear God,

I think that you are wonderful. When you invented snow, did you know that people would use it for skiing?

Love,
Amy
[aged 10]

Dear God,

Next time you send a flood, could you please send me a telegram beforehand? Mostly, I've been good.

Ted
[aged 12]

Dear God,

Do you have a giant computer or do you count all the people of the world on your fingers?

Love,
William
[aged 6]

Dear God,

I am a big fan of yours and Einstein's, God.
I think that you are both very smart.
But he made bombs and you try to stop them.
That is better.

Jan
[aged 10]

Dear God,

Why didn't you make cars earlier, God? That way the Jews could have good speed and gotten away from the Egyptians' land faster and David could have made a clean get away from Goliath.

Theresa
[aged 9]

Dear God,

Do you feel that the scientists and the presidents are to blame for nuclear weapons or are you willing to take on the responsibility yourself?

Jerome
[aged 12]

Mr. God,

I think it is amazing the way everything fits together in the world. Look at heat in our houses, the moon, the sun and rain so farmers' plants will grow.

How do you do it? Mirrors?

Judy
[aged 11]

Dear God,

Volcanos are cool. But you should learn to control your temper (that is what my mother always says to me).

Love,
Victor
[aged 11]

Dear God,

I learned that when it is 1 o'clock here it is a different time in China. Why? Did you want to keep us guessing?

Sincerely,
Ellen
[aged 9]

God,
   Is a hail storm a big God sneeze? Bless you.
                         Terrence
                         [aged 8]

Dear God,
   Thank you for all the great food that we can grow.
   My two favorite foods are watermelon and ice cream
(rocky road).
   It would be great if by 2000, we could grow ice cream (at
least vanilla, chocolate, and rocky road).
   If you are planning on making some changes that would
be a good one.
                         Love,
                         Mel
                         [aged 10]

GOD
God's Lab
   Earth to God. Earth to God. Come in God.
   POW. POW.
   Hey God. Let's play making things. Let's make a radar
station. Then let's make a new kind of plane. it will have
supersonic hearing. That way it can catch hijackers. They
will have to report to the devil then.
                         Tim
                         [aged 10]

Dear God,

What I want to know is – where do people go when they die? My dad says you go to Russia if you're not good. I don't think so because it's too cold there.

Yours truly,
Andrew
[aged 9]

Dear God,

I think it's unbelievable the way you made thunder and lightning bolts. We like the way you make lightning bolts so much, we put them on our football uniforms! I play for the Chargers.

Dan
[aged 11]

Dear God,

I'm in the fifth grade and we have to do a science fair project. We can get help from a grownup (honest). I think maybe you would be ok. Can you help me out?

Diane
[aged 11]

Dear God,

I heard that you can predict the future. Are you better than a horoscope? What do you think I'm going to ask for next Christmas?

Best wishes,
Susan
[aged 11]

Dear God,

I love you. I love the way you made the sky and the sun.

One thing I wondered though. Doesn't it get kind of hot up there near the sun?

We are air conditioned so we are OK.

Love,
Deirdre
[aged 8]

To God,

My question is this one. Did you create all the oceans at once or add when you needed it?

Was the Pacific hard to do?

Ronny
[aged 8]

Dear God,
Have you ever wondered if you made a mistake?
Do you think maybe it would have been better to do babies different?
I mean look at all the trouble it has made.

Let me Know,
Leon
[aged 12]

'Is That Khadaffi Guy
like Pharoah in the Bible?'

Dear God,

I am Jewish and I have visited the state of Israel three times.

My dad says that Jews and Arabs are cousins.

I have a question for you.

If Jews and Arabs are supposed to be cousins, how come they can't get along?

I get along better with my cousin Riva better than that.

Love,
Sylvia
[aged 9]

Dear Mr God,

Why don't you have girls fight in wars? Even in the Bible they didn't. You'd think that because they are hard to get along with, they would be good at fighting!

Marty
[aged 10]

Dear God,

I thought Rambo was dumb. Please stop the wars so we don't have any more of this.

Curt
[aged 8]

Dear God,

I want to suggest a thing.

More Peace!

While I have your attention, I would also like to ask for a pair of Reebok sneakers for Christmas.

Thank you,
Caroline
[aged 11]

Dear God,

Please make all the people on the earth better to each other. That means no more terrorism and violence like on tv.

I want to say thanks for that you are trying to do.

Best wishes,
Anita
[aged 11]

Dear God,

Why did you make it so there is always two sides to things, good guys and bad guys, east and west? We are all the same. Aren't we?

Truly,
Ken
[aged 12]

Dear God,

When I grow up will I have to fight in the army? Will there be a war?

I'm not chicken or anything. I just want to know in advance.

Terry
[aged 10]

Dear God,

Was there a China in your day? Did you know Marcus Polo?

Ted
[aged 8]

Dear God,

I read about what the Turks did to the Armenians a long time ago. That wasn't nice. I'm Armenian.

Garo
[aged 8]

Dear God,

Do you try to avoid Russia when you travel?

Love,
Sharon
[aged 7]

Dear God,
  Is that Khadaffi guy like Pharoah in the Bible or is he worse?

                              Alex
                              [aged 8]

Dear God,
  I think that President Reagan is like my grandfather but my grandfather is nicer. Did you vote for Reagan?
                              John
                              [aged 7]

Dear God,
  My family and me went to Germany last summer. We stopped at those camp places were a lot of people died.
  My question is – did you know about this? Were you away then?

                              Please answer when you
                              can,
                              Cindy Ellen
                              [aged 11]

Dear God,
  The bomb is not such a hot invention. Maybe you should recall it.
                              Love,
                              Margaret
                              [aged 12]

Dear God,

My family and I are practicing Catholics. The stuff in North Ireland bothers us a lot. I don't know if your Irish or not. Maybe you could help though.

Sincerely,
Kathleen
[aged 10]

Dear General God,

Boy, you sure do have a lot of wars here. We learned in history about World Wars I and II. Then there was the Korean war. I don't know much about that. Then there was Vietnam. Now there always seem to be some fighting going on.

I figure we must be sergeants to you. You must want things this way. Otherwise it would not have been like that in the Bible too. And there was plenty of WAR there too.

Andy
[aged 10]

Dear God,

That was a cool trick with the slingshot.

Dave
[aged 10]

Dear God,

Could you talk to the Sikhs and Hindus. I am Hindu but I live in America. I have family far away. I don't want to see them harmed.

In case you don't know, America is not too far from Canada.

With love and kindness,
Mahua
[aged 9]

Dear God,

I saw a poster in a store that went like this:
WAR IS BAD FOR KIDS AND OTHER LIVING THINGS LIKE THAT

As a kid i feel it is my duty to tell you about this. If you have not seen it you should. You can get it at Woolworth's.

Sandy
[aged 10]

Dear Jesus,

Are we related?

My two uncles have beards. Maybe we are. (They are in the army though.)

Love,
Francine
[aged 7]

Dear God,

At church my minister talks a lot about throwing stones and sins. Any idea what he means?

I think you must know. I don't get the hang of this stuff.

A regular church-goer,
Artie
[aged 11]

'Is There a Christmas
in Russia, God?'

Dear God, Jesus, Mary, or who ever is there,

I have always wondered. Do people in far off places like Syria and Arabia have Christmas?

If they do not what do they think they are doing when they eat turkey and stuffing and sing carols.

Happy New Years,
Troy
[aged 7]

Dear God,

What do bunnies have to do with Easter?
Why don't you have camels instead?

I will let you know if I think of anything else to do.
Brian
[aged 10]

Dear Santa,

I was going to write God but I heard that you were in charge of toys.

Love ♡ ♡ ♡
Brooke
[aged 6]

Dear God,
   We learned in school about a book called the koran. Do they do that one at Easter Vigil or something?
                              Charlotte
                              [aged 12]

Dear God,
   Do you have a Christmas tree or a whole (maybe holy) forest? It must be hard to light it all up.
                              Danny
                              [aged 9]

Dear Jesus,
   I want to thank you for going up there on the Cross for us every Good Fridays.
   You must be really happy when the weekend is over.
                              Anita
                              [aged 11]

Dear God,
   Easter is eggsactly what I would have created.
                              Loren
                              [aged 11]

Dear God,
    My favorite Christmas song is Rudolf.
    What's yours?
    I bet you like jingle bells. That one is a lot older.
                                    Jordan
                                    [aged 6]

Dear God,
    Here is five things I would like to see changed.
    Number 1 – Mass
    Number 2 – Bad nuns
    Number 3 – War
    Number 4 – Television
    Number 5 – Make Christmas every week
                                    Donny
                                    [aged 12]

Dear God,
    Was Jesus born in a manger because there was no Holiday
Inns in those years?
                                    Ricky
                                    [aged 10]

Dear Special Person,
    Thank you for Christmas, Easter, and for summer. Also
thanks for being with me.
    My next birthday is July 16. Mark it down.
                                    Ryan
                                    [aged 7]

DEAR God,
   Did you put All Saints Day near Holloween to give all the sides an equal chance? Hah hah.

> I am going to be a monk on Holloween.
> Fitz
> [aged 11]

Dear God,
   What is franks and cents? Was it an old kind of money?

> Maybe it was food?
> Todd
> [aged 7]

Dear God,
   In the Holy Land, what do you do about snow for Christmas? That must be different and kind of weird.

> Bobby
> [aged 9]

Dear God,
   Is there a Christmas in Russia?
   They got nerve. They must have stole it from us.

> Jimmy K.
> [aged 11]

Dear Sky God,
  Do you have holidays on the moon?
  I bet you eat lots of cheese there with dinner.
                              Captain Kirk
                              [aged 12]

Santa Claus, the reindeer, and God,
  I am going to catch you. I am going to make you stay for
cereal and milk.
  I like Lucky Charms. You can have Cherios. Rudolph can
have red cereal.
                              Alex
                              [aged 5]
My mom helped me spell this.

Dear God,
  I know my mother and father give the things on Xmas,
but I still think you must be the inspiration.
  Thanks. Keep giving them ideas.
                              Yours truly, at Xmas and
                              always,
                              Danielle
                              [aged 12]

Dear God,
  What is a Greek Orthodox?
  I hear they have a different year than we have. How can
that be?

Do you cover them too?

Felicia

[aged 10]

Dear God,

Is it a big letdown for you after Christmas? What about Santa?

What do you do on new years eve and the day too? Or is that old hats to you buy now after a million years?

Carlton

[aged 10]

Dear God,

I think it is really cool the way you made such a big day for your son and had the whole world give gifts and all. But I think you should be fair and have days for the apostels too.

Petermas   Paulmas   Andymas

Even Judasmas would be good. Everyone should get a chance.

Merry Christmas,

Andy

[aged 11]

Dear God,

You are the best.

Easter is the best holiday.

Jesus's resurrection is the best story. I saw it in a movie once. It was the best vampire movie I ever saw.

Love,

Arn

[aged 7]

Dear God,

I am Lutheran and two of my best friends are Jewish. One other is different all together. He is from India.

I think that it is not right that you left them out of Christmas. Please put them back in. They are very kind to me.

Ann
[aged 9]

'Could You Please Change
the Taste of Asparagus, God?'

Dear God,
    Do you have telephones in heaven? My number is 555-6392. What is yours? I get home from school about three-thirty everyday.

                                        Martha
                                        [aged 8]

Dear Creator,
    I think the best thing you ever invented was cartoons. All the kids I know love 'em.

                                        Dan
                                        [aged 7]

Dear God,
    My dad drinks beer. It looks kind of gross.
    Did King Solomon drink beer?

                                        Stanley
                                        [aged 10]

Dear God,
    DON'T GIVE UP ON US AND WE WON'T FORGET ABOUT YOU.

                                        Anonymous
                                        [aged 11]

Dear God, Mary, and Family,

Merry Christmas to all of you and all your relatives. That means Jesus and Peter too.

> Love,
> Cynthia Sykes
> 12 Treadmill Road
> [aged 7]

To God/ Send it Federal Express

Hope this gets to you by 1999. Otherwise I get my stamp back. Guaranteed!

> Dawn
> [aged 11]

Dear God,

I have doubts about you sometimes. Sometimes I really believe. Like when I was four and I hurt my arm and you healed it up fast. But my question is, if you could do this why don't you stop all the bad in the world? Like war. Like diseases. Like famine. Like drugs.

And there are problems in other people's neighborhoods too.

> I'll try to believe more,
> Ian
> [aged 10]

Dear God,

I wish I could spend all my time with you. We could go to beautiful places together. Like Paris. We could fill all the world with love. We could make every kid and grownup smile.

I don't think you can do it alone. Why don't you make me a special helper? My family and my teachers will understand. I am willing to give up some kids' stuff. It will be for a very good cause. How about it?

> With all the love in my heart,
> Marti
> [aged 9]

P.S. I would like to take my
pink and white dress
with me, if that is okay.

Dear God,

What do you think of kings and queens like Prince Charles and Queen Di?

I think they are snobs, if you ask me.

> Ernie
> [aged 11]

Dear God,

Can you get me into a soap opera?

> Love and kisses,
> Betty
> [aged 8]

Dear God in heaven,

Thank you so much for helping my two years old brother stop peaing in his pants. My whole family is relieved!

Thank you,
Lorissa
[aged 6]

Dear 'God,'

How did you get the name Earth? Ever think of changing it?

I'd like to see it called Tom's World.

Tom
[aged 11]

Dear God,

Do you believe in spirits and ghosts? What about things in outer space? I don't but my friend Ed says their all around. I think Ed is weird.

Robert
[aged 11]

Dear God,

Could you change the taste of asparagus? Everything else is OK.

Love,
Fred
[aged 9]

Dear Big God,
I think that you look like a big monster. But you do good things for people. Like feasts and famine.

You make me laugh,
Diane
[aged 10]

Dear God,
My mother said we used to eat fish on Fridays. Did you stop it because of the smell?

Very truly yours,
Christa
[aged 11]

Dear God and Jesus,
I'm a big follower of you guys. I root for you both all the time. Keep those miracles coming.

Stephen
[aged 8]

To Whom It May Concern,
I want to believe in you real hard. But I don't know how. My mom does but my dad does not. How can I know for sure? Why don't you make things easier? It would be nice. Nothing special. You don't have to part the sea or nothing. Just something easy.

Like have me turn thirteen sooner.

> Joan
> [aged 12]

Dear God,

I saw the Grand Canyon last summer. Nice piece of work.

> Love,
> Alan
> [aged 9]

Dear GOD,

I think that you are very kind and generous.
Can you see if I can get a bigger allowance?

> Mike
> [aged 11]

Dear God,

I don't really believe in you but I'm supposed to write a letter so here goes.

Also I want to get in a book.

If you are real why don't you prove it by appearing to me? I'll be on Schoolhouse Road at 5 O'CLOCK tomorrow. We'll see.

> Laura
> [aged 9]

Dear Lord,
    You and I have something in common.
    We both have a lot of names.
    You have Lord
            God
            Jesus
            Father.

                            Signed,
                            Rodney William Peter
                            Johnson, Junior
                            [aged 8]

Dear God,
    In school we read all there about Jesus being born.
    One part I did not understand.
    What is a mackulet decepsion?

                            Love,
                            Phyllis
                            [aged 10]

Dear Only God,
    You light up my life. So do mom and dad.

I hope you like this.   Luv,
I am not sure what it   Toni
means.   [aged 7]

Dear God,

Thank you for sending Doctor Heller to ask me questions about you. He is very nice and we are becoming friends now.

But he looks too young to be a doctor. He looks more like an actor.

Maybe he was in a Bible movie.

Love,
Connie
[aged 10]

Dear God,

I read that home is where God (that's you) is.

What does that mean, I wonder?

Does it mean if I am at religious school I am not away from home?

Do I have to be in our living room to be with you?

Are you everywhere?

I am not sure. I just know that you are in my heart.

David
[aged 12]